The Nomadic Notebook – Norway

The Nomadic Notebook – Norway

True short stories of travel adventures and encounters

Daniel Purdy

CONTENTS

CONTENTS

Jesper,

Your patience and willingness to teach a man lost in the woods irreversibly changed my life for the better. I can never return to how I was, and the mountains, oceans, and forests shine bright with adventure, thanks to you. You unearthed my explorer's soul, and everything that has followed is due to you. Thank you, my friend.

PREFACE

On a chilly, blustery Autumn 2015 day in Duluth, Minnesota, I found myself sitting at my desk, the ideal image of an up-and-coming aerospace engineer. Clean shaven, freshly ironed button-up shirt, and proudly displaying a colorful piece of fabric for Tie-Tuesday. But something was missing; I wasn't working at all. Instead, my face was crinkled with consternation and concentration. Consternation as I pondered my dark and musty cubical and concentration as I read an online article describing a freelance writer's journey to traveling full-time and exploring the world. The article wasn't specific, hardly a How-To guide, and more of an overview of this writer's new life. But something clicked in my mind, and I decided then to make a similar change.

Years later, I'm writing these words with a couple weeks' worth of scruff transitioning towards a fledging beard while watching a young trotter horse named *Survivor* paw at the ground in her enclosure as she tries to coax more hay out of us – and all with an icy Norwegian spring rain pelting the window. This current trip to Norway, in particular, seems to bring the previous several years full circle. That time included Scotland,

Nicaragua, Chile, Peru, Argentina, Honduras, Nepal, and this original country I visited all those years ago after leaving my engineering career – Norway.

Between learning the basics of horse and farm care on our current adventure, I find myself reminiscing deeply about that first adventure. That inaugural trip where I, by and large, encountered the world outside a technical Midwest career for the first time, and it changed my life forever. Therefore, now is as good a time as any to put those experiences on paper, as much for my own remembrances as for your enjoyment. So, every experience and story that follows actually happened and is, to the best ability of my memory, true.

Every person who has ever taken a trip to a far-off destination has their own method of categorizing that experience. Very few of us retain every detail, sight, taste, and sound. Instead, our recollections focus on highlights. Happenings that, somehow, earned their spot in our memories and can immediately be summoned when we remember moments in far-away places.

These highlights vary from traveler to traveler. Some may recall amazing landscapes, buildings, and similar images they had the privilege to see. Others may remember emotions, the thrill of exploring a new city, or the uncertainty of navigating an unknown language. But for me, it's the people.

Every place I have been and street I've navigated started as a greyscale portrait, and the people I've met have added color. They've evoked every flavor of emotion imaginable on my travels, from gut-wrenching hilarity to solemn reflection. I have no recollection of traveling without someone nearby who played a crucial role in that memory.

My goal is to relate these people to you, and in so doing, paint a picture of the world as I experienced it with their help. That first corner of the world was northern Norway, just off the coast of the tiny village of Nordskot.

The World Opens

Growing up in the Midwest, we had neither mountains nor big water, and I was always awed by the majesty of both when I saw them. As I flew into Northern Norway on a crisp, clear June morning, it seemed that the ocean and mountains were the last two pieces of some titanic puzzle, and in a fit of impatience, they were smashed together to finish the work.

Looking out to the west, the ocean curved gracefully into the distance, wrapped in its velvety cloak of blue. Calming and mysterious as big water often is. But suddenly, as my eyes drifted eastward, a massive black and grey stone behemoth forcefully thrust itself into the picture, pushing the water to either side to steal the stage as it soared thousands of feet into the sky. The water began to serpentine in haphazard directions beyond this outer sentry, fighting for its place while dodging more mountains suddenly appearing in droves. These mountains soon began joining together to form the outer tendrils of the coast, herding the ocean into the famous fjords of the region. I'd never seen mountains and sea in such an interlocked embrace, where the cliffs and walls of the mountains would plunge straight into the vividly turquoise ocean without pause.

The rugged picture in front of me easily held my attention and slowly began to turn my trepidation into anticipation. My fear was easy to trace. I'd never traveled alone before, anywhere. Yet, I'd left English announcements behind two airports ago and was hurdling toward a new country where a complete stranger had agreed to host me at his fledging island lodge in exchange for my willingness to pull my weight and help where I could. What did a midwestern engineer know of Norwegian island life anyway? It may sound like a blind leap of faith, but it felt more like a blind, deaf, and incredibly dumb tumble into the unknown with no backup plan and little resembling a primary plan. Nevertheless, that daunting landscape glimpsed from the airplane rekindled that spark of excitement that set me on this path over a year ago. The sort of naive excitement borne of whim and inexperience, and although I knew in the back of my mind that I was unprepared and clueless to what was coming, I was ready to push through the door of imagination and experience it for myself.

No matter what lay ahead, that magical landscape called for exploration. I pictured myself paddling into misty fjords or climbing up those rock faces, and a slow grin involuntarily spread across my face. I'd stay as long as my visa allowed; that was already decided before the plane wheels touched the tarmac.

A short ferry ride brought me even closer to those giant stone sentries that had caught my attention from the air. But now I could hear the waves crashing against their stout shoulders and feel the sharp spring wind whip across the Arctic Ocean. I shivered as I burrowed deeper into my thick coat and regretted not purchasing an international phone plan to check in with my potential host as I thought to myself, *I sure hope this guy exists.*

"You must be Dan. I'm Jesper", the apparent model for Viking life stated in only slightly accented English as he crossed the sizable pier in what seemed like two strides. Standing well above seven feet, festooned with a full black beard and tousled black hair, I wasn't sure whether I should smile at the walking stereotype or be slightly intimidated.

But his comfortable grey sweater, matching knee-high rubber boots, and a friendly smile won the day. I took his outstretched hand and confirmed that I was indeed the latest volunteer to join his ranks in this corner of remote Norway. I immediately noted his rough and calloused hand and made a mental note that my goal to exchange my soft desk life for practical hard work was likely about to pay dividends.

"We'll head off to the island when I get these people sorted," he continued, gesturing to the group of four or five Norwegians who had disembarked from the ferry with me. Until now, I'd given the boisterous group plenty of space. After all, they clearly belonged here, whereas I was just as obviously an outsider. From their accepted wardrobe of loose, knitted sweaters and sturdy rubber boots to their confident yet slightly grizzled faces, they were the complete antithesis of the interloper that had stepped off the ferry behind them.

My shiny new Eddie Bauer duffle, habitually shaved face, and preppy clothing – selected by one who expected to encounter the outdoors without knowing exactly how to dress for it – all screamed "clueless tourist." But we all were now apparently bound for the same island lodge where I would spend the next several months volunteering. So, it seemed that some interaction with the locals was probably called for. But my quiet and introverted self – which hadn't spoken to a soul since leaving Minneapolis – was going to need some prodding, and Jesper was more than happy to oblige.

With a friendly bellow of recognition, Jesper turned from me to move towards the guests. I vaguely worried about the structural integrity of the old wooden pier as I felt it tremble beneath me with each step. But it held firm, and I turned my attention to the village arrayed in front of me to pass the time as Jesper administered the Norwegian pleasantries. The first word that popped into my mind was 'trim.' Comprised of only a pair of streets, the couple dozen houses arranged along the bay splashed colors of barnyard red, dijon mustard, and Grecian blue across the otherwise gray and whites of the early spring landscape that had yet to see any notable green growth. The houses seemed maintained, the street was clean, and the whole village – which was so small not even to be worthy of a Wikipedia page – was without any fluff. Very trim.

More eye-catching, however, was the backdrop of mountains and cliffs directly behind the village that appeared to shield this place from the rest of the world. To the south sat Sørskottinden mountain, and extending north from that mountain was the Nordskot Traverse. A long sheer cliff extending about half a mile northward in a crescent shape until it connected to the next peak. This impressive fixture, therefore, had the appearance of a massive defensive wall flanked by skyrocketing guard towers that would have made even a titan feel shielded.

Nestled within this natural fortress, the tiny town of Nordskot, with its single general store/post office, seemed almost insignificant. But at that moment, it was my new home, and I couldn't have been more pleased. Far away from the hustle of the world that I was trying desperately to escape, and overflowing with opportunities for adventure, I could finally give a definitive nod of my head and know with certainty, I'd arrived.

I was brought back from my revelry as Jesper made a general announcement in Norwegian, and the guests then began shuffling towards a compact motorboat tied up to the pier. He then turned my way and asked if I'd help get the guests into the boat and untie the mooring lines. My Midwest politeness kicked in immediately, and I agreed to help without the slightest inkling of how to complete the task. Nevertheless, I hopped into the boat with more gusto than grace, tossed my bags into the least damp corner, turned, and began taking the bags half-offered, half-thrown as the guests tried their best to avoid leaning too far over the icy arctic water between pier and boat.

In the front of the boat, Jesper crossed over from the pier as smoothly as stepping down from a curb. However, no matter the grace in the act, the craft gave a definitive lurch. I'd never needed a boat nor shipboard balance to tack in and out of traffic on the Minneapolis highway. A deficiency brought into sharp focus as the boat's sudden movement nearly sent me pitching headfirst into the blue waters of the Arctic while clutching a guest's bag.

I thankfully had the presence of mind, or sheer survival instinct, to fling out a hand that caught the edge of the pier several feet in front of me. For a moment, I was trapped, my hand grasping a slippery wooden pier, head and shoulders suspended above oblivion, and everything from hips down desperately trying not to slip out of the boat. I immediately cursed my overzealous helpfulness and that I'd already loosened one of the mooring lines as I felt my thighs scrape against the edge of the boat as it inched away from the pier. A quick push-off from the slimy dock and I tumbled back into the vessel's stern and gingerly laid the guest's bag next to the others.

Glancing Jesper's way with an apology already forming in my mind, I saw his big black beard split into a smirk that my steep learning curve would often elicit in the coming months. So I sheepishly stepped aside for the guests to jump into the boat and reserved myself to planning how I would improve my boat etiquette over the next few months.

After a five-minute ride to the island, the process was repeated in reverse as the guests and baggage were unloaded. This was evidently not their first visit as they quickly thanked Jesper for the pickup – at least, I assumed that's what the melodic Norwegian equated to – and started making their way to their cabins unassisted. Jesper just as quickly started leading me around the crescent-shaped dock, past a couple of rowboats, a sleek trimaran as glossy as a pearl, and around to a large white house.

The crescent pier was eighty percent wood planking, tracking about five hundred feet around a relatively deep and protected cove that formed the northern tip of our little two-acre island. There were two docks in this little cove. The largest jutted straight into the water from the center of the crescent, and we had moored our boat here. This larger dock joined the shore-bound boardwalk that turned right to a series of beautiful glass-walled cabins cantilevered over the icy arctic water. All the guests had wandered in this direction. But we headed left, down a set of stairs and across a short sandy beach before the boardwalk again sprang from the rock and supported a second, smaller dock that also doubled as a porch for the quaint little white cabin that sat just a few feet from the icy water's edge.

While walking, he explained that the house was one of the only original buildings left after the island was developed for the lodge business. Upon quick inspection, I found it had a distinctly cozy appearance as it sat on the uneven rock of the island with the main entrance opening onto the dock, just feet from the icy water with a mountain on the mainland silhouetted behind it. A comfortable haven in an imposing environment, I thought.

As far as houses go, this one meshed perfectly with those tidy examples I'd seen in the village and spotted on the many nearby islands. White wood sidings, matching white trim, and a dark grey roof on the two-story frame. Nothing extraordinary, but it was everything I could wish for. Until then, all my pent-up hopes to shake my life loose from a constraining cubicle were abstract aberrations. Vague and swirling thoughts about what I'd like to shape my life to be, without concrete knowledge or experience on which to build that life. But at that moment, the quaint cabin framed by an imposing Norwegian mountain with the turquoise blue-green arctic ocean only feet away was the evidence I needed to realize what my life could be and that I was ready to start building it right here. At that instant, I knew my seven-month leave of absence from desk-based engineering had just been extended to a lifetime, and my life was indeed about to change drastically and permanently.

And the catalyst for that life change was lumbering next to me as we approached the black front door. Jesper, I'm sure, had no idea of the monumental role he was about to play in changing my life. Nor did my fellow volunteers, who I was about to be introduced to.

2

Sheepish Pursuits

I had traveled to Norway to "expand my knowledge and experiences beyond that of a desk," according to my lovingly crafted request for a leave of absence from engineering. To learn skills I'd never needed before, complete tasks as foreign as the language, and simply see a new side of the world and myself. To that end, helping run an island lodge in Arctic Norway did not disappoint, and Jesper flung me into an endless array of tasks without delay.

Compost trenches needed to be dug, mucky soil drained, supplies fetched from the mainland (after a bumpy and exhilarating introduction to boat piloting), cabins cleaned, and the list continued to match tasks that were entirely new to me. But in exchange for a few hours of work several days a week, Jesper and his partner Astrid offered three daily meals and a bed in the volunteer cabin that had already taken first place among my favorite spots in the world.

However, I wasn't learning and completing these island tasks alone. Other travelers from around the world routinely passed through to contribute their skills and perhaps acquire some new ones in the process. I often envied these more skilled and experienced volunteers as an ex-engineer had little to contribute to Nordic island life, but there was endless opportunity to learn here.

Jozef from France was one such comrade. As a past carpenter, Jozef's skills were crucial to Jesper's plan of restoring a neglected hut on the island to a comfortable cabin for future volunteers. I, therefore, almost always saw Jozef's wiry frame festooned with tool belts, hammers, and tape measures while his curly black hair sported a faint highlight of tan sawdust.

His English wasn't fluent, but he was undoubtedly conversational – and his favorite phrase was "everything is under control." However, when seasoned with his French accent, all I heard shouted from his work area after a loud crash was, "Ever-sing is oonder controol!"

Or when he dropped a dish in the volunteer house. Or asked how his day was going. The answer was always the same. "Ever-sing is oonder controol."

At perhaps five-foot-five, Jozef wasn't the giant gregarious handyman portrayed by Duluth Trading Company ads. He was almost the antithesis of the large burly carpenter often stereotyped in America. But his slender frame slid up and down that hut's roof, often carrying obscenely heavy loads of lumber, while his perpetual black scruff sealed his stature as a heavily skilled individual.

But Jozef's almost daily dance through sawdust, hammer blows, and colorful French vulgarity wasn't completely isolated. He often attracted the unerring attention of our island's small sheep flock. Their usual flat grassy haunt in the island's center bordered Jozef's project, tucked into the only small thicket of trees we had. And there they'd stand, watching and occasionally munching on the tough greenery like spellbound spectators enjoying overly buttered popcorn at the theater.

The six or seven bouncing lambs recently joining this flock also added to their theater patronage. Frolicking and darting here and there with no regard for the enrapturing show that their parents seemed to believe Jozef was performing.

One specific lamb stood out from the rest, and it was more than his distinctive jet-black right ear and snowy white left. It was the fact that neither of those ears was tagged. Our volunteer predecessors had found themselves one ear tag short for this particular youngster. The ear tag in question – think of it as your vehicle registration sticker but for livestock – was ponderously working its way through the Norwegian postal service to our remote enclave. In the meantime, our young charges continued to grow until they progressed from bouncing, bumbling lambs to lightning-fast juveniles darting from one end of the island to the other with ease, always keeping their parents within sight, who – in turn – never seemed to let Jozef's labors out of theirs.

But this close observation went both ways, and Jozef soon became thoroughly acquainted with these wooly organic lawnmowers. That's why his surprisingly mighty bellow of laughter was the first thing we heard when Jesper informed us that the tag had finally arrived during our daily chore talk one clear July morning.

"We never catch them," Jozef stated succinctly once his laugh subsided, his eyes growing extra wide to emphasize the point that his English vocabulary couldn't quite express, "so fast!"

Jesper rolled his eyes skyward as his big black beard cracked into a grin. "There's four of you. Surely you can catch just one sheep." He raised one of his oar-sized fingers to emphasize the point. But he only saw wary glances jump between me, Jozef, Nikolai, and Jonas.

Nikolai, a powerfully built CrossFitter from Denmark, had only recently arrived on the island and hadn't yet reached the level of familiarity to voice his opinion. But I noticed his eyebrows tick up towards his close-cropped dark blonde hair and his full beard crease into a frown. From a brief dabble with CrossFit back home, I knew that most of its acolytes detested any form of running, and that disdain was written all over Nikolai's face as he considered chasing a lamb all over the island.

Jonas, on the other hand, was never one to hold back his opinion. This second Dane had been my work partner for weeks as we installed a drainage pipe on the island, and his daily surf through puns, jokes, and antics had sealed his position as the island prankster. These characteristics were complemented by a face that could drift from complete seriousness to the widest, toothiest grin I've ever seen and eyes that appeared to howl with laughter. Those eyes twinkled now as he said, "How about you come running with us?"

We'd all learned by now that our towering giant of a host loathed anything faster than a hike. As I remembered that fact, Jesper's arm seemed to telescope across the room as he gave Jonas a friendly smack on the back of the head, and I made a mental note to never doubt the reach of a seven-foot-tall Viking.

"I'm the boss here," Jesper asserted while puffing out his chest enough that I could hear his grey knit sweater creaking in protest. "And besides, wouldn't it be a nice change of pace?"

Jesper's eyes swiveled in Jonas and my direction with this last statement. Our drainage project wasn't exactly exhilarating, and I could still spot a few specks of mud clinging to Jonas's light brown nape-length hair from repeatedly heaving sodden earth over his shoulder. My own callouses, which had until recently been blisters, voiced their agreement, and Jonas and I shared a mutual shrug of agreement.

"Well, there are four of us," I echoed Jesper's earlier statement to show that I was in. Jonas nodded, and Nikolai's blond beard reversed course into a begrudging smile as he agreed.

Josef let out another surprisingly powerful laugh for such a small man and looked to Jesper to speak for all of us, "ever-sing is oonder control."

That's how the four of us ended up marching from the volunteer cabin, turning left to follow the crescent dock along the water, and transiting to the dirt path that showed Jonas's and my recent digging efforts as we turned towards the main two-story building about two hundred feet away at the center of the island.

This main building – which strangely was never given a specific name in my time there – seemed to me brusquely cozy. Plain brown walls on three sides and a full series of windows on the fourth made for a stoic-looking but inviting building. The trend continued indoors, where dull flagstone floors and simple wooden tables worked with tastefully selective decorations to create an appealing sense of comfort. A feeling often exemplified by the loaves of fresh sourdough bread that Astrid produced daily. But we passed on the delicious food we could see being laid out for lunch and continued around the building to the flat open field where we knew our charges were waiting.

My own words echoed in my head as we dumbly stood on one end of the field watching the sheep as they stood on the other side warily watching us, like two opposing football teams staring each other down before a match, *four of us and only one sheep to catch*. In hindsight, I knew this was my inner city slicker speaking, who couldn't be further from reality.

That statement was only equaled in its preposterousness by the hilarity of what was about to ensue.

Our multi-national team huddled to formulate a plan, and we started simple. The sheep always stood together, an insight gained by Jozef's frequent observation, so surround the group and slowly close the circle until the sheep began to move and grab the lamb. Simplicity itself.

I could feel a group of island guests observing us from the large windows as they settled in for lunch. *That's typical*, I thought to myself; *no pressure*. Part of me wondered if Jesper had quickly made his trip to the mainland to shuttle guests here just for their amusement as we fanned out to try and encircle the sheep.

The sheep's cold appraisal of our efforts erupted in a lightning sprint before we were ever close to being ready. "That what I say!" Jozef yelled as he took the lead for a dogged foot chase across the island as we tried to overtake the lamb.

We dashed across the center of the island, sprinting by the main building and crossing the dirt from Jonas's and my previous efforts. The sheep turned left as they reached the crescent dock, opting for a gravel path with a jagged rock wall on the left and the turquoise ocean on the right. This path allowed them to thunder past several of the island's cantilevered cabins overlooking the water, whose occupants emerged to watch the proceedings with amused interest.

The sheep appeared well organized and rehearsed for this conflict and careened left at the end of this path in perfect synchronization. They scaled a steep section of rock and disappeared over a small hill leading back to the island's center.

"That way, that way!" shouted Jozef in his sometimes-ponderous French accent, directing Nikolai and me back the way we came for what I perceived to be a flanking maneuver. Jozef and Jonas took off, scrambling up the rock in hot pursuit of the sheep. His constant work ascending and descending his ladder for carpentry work seemed to come in handy, and he flew up the rock as agile as any sheep on their best day and was quickly out of sight.

So, back Nikolai and I ran. Back along the path, waving to the guests as we sprinted back over the drainage area, churning up mud as we went, then around the other side of the hill to where the sheep must have run. But they weren't there. A little more than a football field of mostly open island, and we'd managed to misplace a herd of sheep.

After a minute or two of comically looking around us as if the sheep might perhaps be cleverly dug in and camouflaged nearby, Jozef finally appeared on the hilltop. A simple shrug of the shoulders told us all we needed to know, and we split up in search of our charges.

Nikolai took off towards the slightly wooded section behind the main house. I turned towards our volunteer house to search around the northern beach just beyond – perhaps foil an attempt by the sheep to signal the mainland for reinforcements. I had barely covered half the distance before I heard a shout from the woods and caught sight of Nikolai pelting across the open field toward the cabin path we had just left. His interest in cross-fit seemed to pay dividends as his toned arms and legs pumped in unison. I took off in hot pursuit as I saw Jozef sprinting southward around the opposite side of the rocky hill. The sheep, I assumed, were somewhere on the beach on the island's west side that butted up to the steep hill we were now flanking.

Once again, past the guests we ran as they had, I'm sure, "Yakety Sax" playing in their heads, or at least the Norwegian equivalent to that ditzy saxophone solo. We ran until the trail ended, and we jumped down to the rocky beach and continued along the precarious space between the cliff-like hill and ocean. Then we saw them; the sheep had taken refuge on a small flat section of rock a few feet up from the sea with massive boulders lining the hill behind them. As if by clockwork, Jozef then appeared just beyond them. Impeccable timing. We had them and closed in on our young black-and-white target. But our happiness was short-lived as the sheep barely gave us a glance before prancing up a gap in the boulders and back onto the hill.

By this time, we were all beginning to feel the hopeless giddiness accompanying an impossible task. A task so insurmountable that all you can do is laugh as you throw yourself at it again and again. Laughing at the sheer hilarity of the situation, we once again ran past the guests and back to our freshly churned-up rallying point atop the drainage pipes.

"Okay, new plan," I said, looking at my compatriot's red cheeks and the eager face of a teenage German guest who had decided to aid our pitiful efforts. "Let's try to drive them to the main dock, they'll have water on three sides, and then we can grab the lamb." They all consented, and we again split up in search of our quarry.

An excited cry behind a stone ledge on the island's east side again had us running to put our plan into action. The sheep broke into view as they charged northward, in the general direction of the dock, and behind them ran our German assistant beaming from ear to ear. The rest of us quickly formed a line behind the sheep and once more pelted across the island's center. Yet again, within sight of our delighted guests, who were likely beginning to make wagers.

Nikolai and I thundered along the wooden dock in front of the volunteer house as Jozef headed to the right flank along the beach. The German took the high ground as he scrambled over a small hill, and we all continued to push to the northern tip of the island. The sheep finally pulled up just shy of the ten-foot drop to the ocean and turned to face us, looking for their opening. Jozef took the lead as we closed ranks and slowly moved towards the L-shaped portion of the dock, which trapped the sheep.

We crept closer and closer, crouched low to maximize our reaction time. Then suddenly, the sheep surged forward. The adults led the charge as they lunged for the small gaps between us, leading the way for the lambs. It was a frenzy of leaping, prancing, and charging sheep as they leaped between and over us in a desperate attempt to avoid our flailing arms. I caught sight of our target, making a mad dash for an opening between Nikolai and Jozef, and I was sure he would slip away. But Jozef managed to save the day with a dramatic leap forward in a full outstretched tackle that would have made any NFL professional proud. He caught the lamb in his arms and made a soft landing while gently keeping the lamb off the rocks. The first thing I heard once the melee had ended was, "ever-sing is oonder control."

A quick squeeze of the tag tool, and we'd completed the job. The best part of an hour chasing sheep for about thirty seconds of actual tagging work.

Our attention now swiveled to each other as we appraised what chasing livestock through mud, trees, and across rock yields. We were filthy, scratched, mucky, and probably as grubby of men as that island had ever seen. But as we trudged back to the main building, we laughed. The full, belly-generated guffaws that only challenging situations combined with hilarity could produce. The happiest among us seemed to be Jozef. His curly black hair was flecked with small twigs and pines from crashing through the saplings after the sheep, and his darkly tanned face cracked into a glistening white smile as he recounted our adventure blow-by-blow. While no doubt disappointed that the show was over, the guests laughed and waved as they saw our victorious procession head back indoors to get cleaned up. We then reported our success to Jesper, with the friendly suggestion that the next time he needed a sheep caught, he could grab a net and do it himself.

3

Stein's Guest

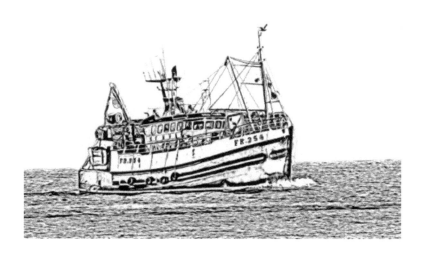

"I'm here for your job, mate," was the only greeting I received when I opened the door to a highly unusual knock at the volunteer cabin. No one ever knocked; we all lived here, so why knock? Moreover, the island guests knew better than to wander into our fiercely guarded haven of irreverent humor and gossip about none other than themselves.

"Um, hi," was all my sputtering brain could think to reply as my internal thoughts raced. *Who's this guy? Is he a guest? Why is he here?*

The serious eyes set behind a thin pair of glasses gave nothing away. "Yeah, I'm moving in," he continued in a heavy English accent as he breezed by me into the living room. I almost melted into the hanging coats while dodging the heavy canvas duffle slung over his shoulder as he passed.

Jonas was the only other volunteer in the cabin at the time. "Um, hi," he echoed my poorly delivered greeting while shooting me a questioning glance.

All I could do was send my shoulders up and mouth corners down in clear bewilderment as our newcomer unloaded his bags and offered himself a seat at the table next to the kitchen – sitting with his back to the wall and table between himself and us, like a stern principle eyeing misbehaving students from behind a sturdy desk. He certainly didn't look like the hardy island type. Standing a few inches shy of six feet, with close-cropped hair in the early stages of recession, small-rimmed spectacles, and a comfortably padded build, he looked more akin to a university librarian than the hardy island folk I'd grown accustomed to.

"Yeah," he continued breathlessly, as if delivering remarkable news. "I'm taking all your jobs." He gestured grandly to both Jonas and me, "and I'm moving in."

The librarian continued to stare us down, his grave eyes giving nothing away. Over this newcomer's shoulder, I saw a dark mass move past the window, so tall that the face was hidden above the window frame. That could only be Jesper.

Moments later, Jesper indeed materialized in our entranceway. He seemed to fill that entire doorframe as he stooped to enter the room. "All good then?" he asked our newcomer, who replied with a simple smile and nod as he kept his eyes on us. I noticed a slight crinkle spreading from behind his glasses.

Jesper turned to us, "Seems like you've already met Antony."

We slowly and suspiciously nodded in unison as our guest chimed in, "just Ant is good."

"Ant ... Ant, Ant," Jesper rolled the name around like he was sampling some exotic wine before continuing. "He's going to be our new chef."

Jonas and I noticeably decompressed as we both vented a pressurized "ohhhh," and cracked into sheepish smiles as Ant finally laughed.

"Your faces!" He cackled, settling comfortably into his chair as the solemn look in his eyes and stern set of his shoulders melted away. Clearly, he had amused himself considerably, and that was enough for him.

Jesper looked curiously between the three of us as he continued. "Ant used to be a chef at Everest Base Camp."

Our eyes continued their journey from suspicious to relieved to extreme envy. "Ohhh," we said in unison once again as admiration quickly displaced our earlier mistrust.

"Aren't you two the perfect chorus," Ant chided our monosyllabic responses. But he brushed away Jesper's compliment and our unasked questions by returning to the matter at hand. "So, where should I put the bags."

"Yes, Jesper," I echoed, slightly peeved that he didn't bother to share his plans for a new addition to the Island. "Where *should* he put his bags?" It was a combined rib and challenge, as I knew Jesper was aware that our little cabin was already bursting at the seams. In fact, the little two-bedroom house was occupied by no less than 6 full-time residents, plus occasionally the lodge's owner if he happened to materialize on the island.

Part of me wanted to poke Jesper as payback for the shock, but he never batted an eye as he pointed out the cabin's side window to the just-visible stone pier. "Stein's going to help us out."

Ant turned his spectacles to me for clarification. "What's a Stein?"

I turned to Jonas in turn, who simply shrugged. Jesper had exquisitely turned the tables on my question, putting me on the spot to answer while he stood expectantly with his hands on his hips. I stared critically at the pier and could barely make out a white-painted mast projecting beyond the dock – almost lost in the overcast skies. A small piece of information that I'd almost entirely disregarded until now finally fluttered to the surface of my mind. "The fishing boat?"

The long crescent dock that formed our cabin's front entranceway continued to the very northern tip of the Island and met a stone pier about a hundred feet after turning right from our front door. The stone pier existed, but its purpose had yet to fully materialize – apart from a convenient pen in which to corral our island's sheep when needed. One day perhaps, it could host full-sized ferries to bring guests to our island instead of relying on the small zippy speedboats (that I oh so enjoyed piloting) to fetch our clientele. But for now, the pier was an empty space with a massive pile of gravel in the middle whose future purpose was never explained to me.

But unfinished as it was, the pier served as a convenient port of call for a local fisherman named Stein, who had negotiated with our host to moor his fishing trawler there on occasion. Stein – meaning "stone" or "rock" in Norwegian – lived up to his name in every sense of the word. He was perhaps fifty years old and had made his living as a fisherman in this region for a significant portion of that time. Imagine a grizzled Nordic sailor, and you'll likely perfectly envision Stein. His grey rubber boots, heavily stained dark work trousers, and frayed grey knit sweater all spoke to countless hours trawling these waters. This uniform continued upward to include grizzled grey scruff and grey knit hat that again matched his trade, name, and overall demeanor as a laconic and dry Norwegian fisherman.

His fishing trawler was, therefore, a regular but disregarded sight. Predominately white with sharp red trim, the ship wasn't a tiny hobby craft by any means. At perhaps fifty feet long with an elevated piloting deck and an additional living deck below, this bulky workhorse was designed to scrape a tough living from the unforgiving Norwegian Sea. But for now, half-way through some renovation work and conveniently docked at our Island, Stein agreed that his trawler could become Ant's new digs.

We all shared a little trepidation as we toted Ant's bags on board. The boat was slightly pitching in the ocean swells and delicately creaking against its mooring ropes in protest against being kept from the sea. The tall radio mast and fishing net booms, along with the cluttered and slightly rusty top deck, added to the overall workhorse feel. We stepped over a rusty patch that seemed in the throes of being scraped before a new coat of paint could be applied. It was hardly the homey feeling that a newcomer would hope to find.

But it seemed that Stein was tiring of the fishing life, and his ubiquitous trawler held a secret. Months of hard work had turned the lower decks into an exceptionally comfortable, almost luxurious, guest space that Stein dreamed of renting for sightseeing cruises around the Fjords. Stepping through that hatch to the lower deck seemed a more considerable trans-formation than suddenly arriving in *Narnia*. Newly installed hardwood floors and teak paneling worked in tandem with velvety-rich furnishings to create soft, snug comfort that made all of us land-dwellers jealous. A full kitchen and bar unobtru-sively occupied one corner, while several luxurious tables and padded benches comprised the main sitting area. At the same time, a separate bedroom held a plushy cushioned twin bed.

Despite being removed from the usual bustle – if you could call it that on an island staffed by less than ten people – Ant seemed content to settle into a semi-removed life as he began work. His trademark dry humor was instantly a favorite among both guests and volunteers, and Ant quickly melded into our little island community.

I'd often see him sauntering past our cabin most mornings as he made his way to the main building to start his day preparing lunch. His hands in his pockets and his head tucked down as if lost in the deepest of thought, or perhaps it was a habit developed after hustling through the icy wind to and from the mess tent at Everest Base Camp.

After checking into the kitchen with the accompanying clatter of pots and pans as he arrayed his campaign for the day, Ant was often lost to us until after the last dinner course was served to the island guests that evening. But as consistently as the tide, he'd slowly saunter back along the dock in the evenings while many of us were sprawled in wooden lounge chairs outside our cabin door. He'd often gratefully accept an offered drink and settle into a chair like the ocean settling into our bay until the tide inevitably dragged it back to sea. But no matter how exhausted he was, his mind seemed tirelessly sharp. Those sleepy librarian eyes perfectly camouflaged a jocular side that he'd always unleash on those quiet evenings.

"What did you do today?" was his usual innocuous warm-up of the evening as he looked around the group for a sparring partner on whom to discharge his pent-up humor since sautéing moose meat and simmering fish chowder all day only offered limited outlets for his comedy. But on one particular night, Jesper provided an easy target as he puttered into the harbor with a couple of late-arriving guests.

"Who's that he's with?" Ant asked as he made a grand show of squinting through his glasses, greatly emphasizing his librarian look.

Jonas looked up from contemplating his beer. "Jesper said he was picking up some guests, some famous chef that won a cooking show or something."

This information prodded Ant to lean closer to the white-painted dock railing and give the approaching stranger an even more critical squint through his glasses. "Well, he can fuck right off," he offered as drily as a drought-stricken Arizona mesa.

Utterly contrary to anything I'd expect this professional hospitality chef to say, I chortled into my cider and replied with a sharp and sarcastic reprimand, reminding him to be on his best behavior.

"Look at that thin wanker," he continued in complete and animated disgust. "How can anyone trust a thin chef? I bet everything he cooks is rubbish, and even he doesn't want to eat it."

"You don't have to be thin to cook bad food." Jonas jumped into the ring with an accusatory volley.

Ant turned his attention from the approaching boat and raised an eyebrow. "You'd know bad food; I've seen you eat that brown cheese."

Jonas drew himself up in wide-eyed horror. "But it's the best!"

"Yes, the best diet food since you can't eat it without honking." Ant retorted with his English accent crystalizing on the last word as he referred to vomiting.

Jonas looked to me for support, but I could only shrug in agreement with Ant. Norway's signature caramelized brown cheese was an acquired taste that I was still far from acquiring. He could only sputter in disbelief as he walked down the boat ramp to help tie up Jesper's craft.

As Jesper and this new guest stepped ashore, I couldn't help but agree with Ant's original thought. After all, the target of his displeasure was a shockingly thin man who looked more like a worse-for-wear kitchen broom than a chef. His rail-thin frame was only given some body by his wild black hair that had a deliberately unkempt look to it.

Meanwhile, Ant, looking contented from his verbal spar, sighed like an old wizened sage as he heaved himself out of his chair and plunged his hands into his pockets as he continued his saunter towards his side of the pier.

But on this particular night, he quickly and unexpectedly came back. He looked uncharacteristically flustered and occasionally glanced over his shoulder as if expecting something to materialize behind him.

He greeted us by way of a direct question that almost sounded like an accusation. "Where's my house?" He asked while looking straight at Jonas, who had a reputation as a prankster.

What a ridiculous question, I thought to myself. After all, where could a house go? This train of thought only lasted a split second before I remembered Ant was living on a boat. Indeed, a much more mobile accommodation, and I confirmed his quandary when a quick glance over his shoulder showed that the distinct white mast from Stein's fishing boat was no longer there.

My shrug mirrored Jonas and Nikolai's, and the rest of our international contingent also voiced their ignorance when we moved inside the volunteer cabin to make inquiries. It seemed that Stein, in addition to being a hard-to-miss walking model for crusty fishermen, was also a master of stealth who had managed to surreptitiously land on the Island, power up his massive fishing trawler, and make his getaway without ever being noticed. A masterfully executed commandeering mission that would make any pirate proud. Yet, it was his boat after all, and a phone call from Jesper confirmed that he had some maintenance – albeit poorly communicated – at the main dock on the mainland to attend to.

But in spite of his exhausted state and realization that all his belongings were on board, I watched the agitated flush slowly drain from Ant's face, and the characteristic crinkles reformed behind his glasses. "Well, at least I don't have to worry about my bloody balance when I take a piss tonight. I always think I'm going to pitch headfirst into the ocean."

I gave him a critical look as I remembered he had a functioning head just a few feet from his cabin below deck. But

Ant just smiled at my consternation, "bloody liberating, mate." And walked into the cabin to find himself a bed.

I tried not to look at our regular jumping spot for plunges into the Arctic Ocean just a few meters from where the fishing boat was regularly docked. But the man's humor under pressure was admirable. Perhaps the aspect of Ant's humor that was most endearing was that his only goal seemed to be to entertain himself. Any additional laughs beyond his own were simply icing on the cake, and I came to admire this greatly. Those librarian's eyes never seemed to lose a slightly amused look, as if he found something hilarious, and he was constantly debating whether to tell us or not. And more often than not, he did.

4

Kayaking to the Midnight Sun

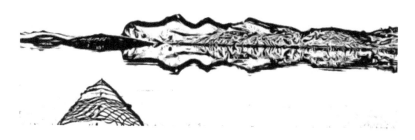

The Arctic Ocean off Nordskot, Norway was one of the greatest dichotomies I'd ever encountered. Splashing the wooden dock just a few steps from our cabin, it was visible from every window and nearly every point on our rocky island, while the briny aroma from the eastern tidal pools was never far away. But its most striking feature was the color. Vivid turquoise currents swirled in the channels between islands while limitlessly deep blues filled the horizon, reminiscent of travel posters to the Caribbean and Southeast Asia. I almost expected tropical birds to frolic overhead or colorful parrotfish to dart between submerged rocks.

But I only needed to stand within a few feet of the water for my musings to be dispelled by the frigid ocean spray. A near-endless march of stiff waves regularly crashed into the island – seemingly sent by the Nordic ocean god Njǫrd himself to correct my foolish daydreaming. This was Nordland, and each wave erupted in a shower of icy needles to remind me of the bone-chilling water temperatures that hovered around forty-five degrees Fahrenheit despite the canvas of tropical color.

Regardless of the shockingly cold water temperatures, the ocean was both highway and livelihood for the hardy residents of this region. Transportation anywhere, be it a neighbor's home or the nearest large city of Bodø, unwaveringly required a boat. Hardened fishermen also trawled the icy water for cod or halibut. At the same time, tour operators offered sightseeing cruises to the nearby Engelvær Nature Preserve or stunning Lofoten Islands, just visible to the north.

Therefore, every soul living in this remote region was innately connected to this stunning ocean – enjoying the remarkable blue-green colors that would make even the showi-est peacock proud while weathering its regular cold and harsh buffeting. But every so often, the sea and wind would tire from the effort of chiseling their way into the fjords and lay back into a pool of perfect calm. On such an occasion, my fellow volunteer, Kelsy, levered her remarkable panache for spontane-ous adventure to persuade me to experience the magic of the arctic ocean illuminated by the midnight sun.

Kelsy was the only other American to join our volunteering team while I was in Norway. Originally from a small North Carolina town, she exemplified the relaxed, we'll get there when we get there, attitude that's often attributed to that part of the country – along with the barely perceptible southern twang of folks caught between Georgia and Maryland. Her bronzed features highlighted her striking white smile, while a slightly rumpled look – as if she had just finished a wild adventure and was ready for another – was ever-present in the form of an off-balance shirt collar or half-tucked-in shirt.

All these endearing characteristics combined to form a carefree individual who was more than happy to follow life wherever it took her and leap at any opportunity to explore beyond the path. Therefore, she was excellent company during the day-to-day work on the island. Our previous day's task of re-securing bumpers to our boats to prevent the constant waves from tearing them loose was enjoyable and nostalgic as we discussed home and favorite music – a conversation that has led to my longtime enjoyment of Lake Street Dive.

But on this particular warm July evening, the ocean took a breath. Barely a ripple creased the ocean's glassy surface all day, and what few trees and shrubs dotted the island stood perfectly still without the faintest breeze. Deprived of the regular crash of waves or wind, the only sound that reverberated around the island was Jozef's occasional hammer blow or shouted French curse as he continued to work on his roofing project on the other side of the island.

In the cozy volunteer cabin, however, Kelsy closely inspected our scheduling whiteboard while I lounged on the sofa beside the friendly wood-burning stove.

"Who wants to go kayaking tonight?" She asked the house at large.

A mumbled deferment drifted down from the upstairs loft, presumably from Nikolai, who I suspected was sleeping in that morning. Another negative response came from Lydia – an English volunteer from Manchester – who was making breakfast in the kitchen.

Kelsy's eye then swiveled on me after finishing her schedule inspection. "You're free tonight." It was a statement, invitation, and confirmation all at once.

"I'm helping Antony serve dinner to the guests tonight." I lamely replied, referring to the island's infinitely entertaining English chef.

"But you're done at eight, and it's not like the sun ever sets." Kelsy already knew I'd be out there in a kayak; she just had to guide me to that conclusion.

I had to grant her that point about the sun. After all, when was the ocean this calm? And when am I ever somewhere with twenty-four-hour sunlight in such beautiful landscapes? I had no excuse or desire to miss out on this particular adventure, so I assented, and we adjourned until the evening.

Recall that our volunteer house sat to one side of a long crescent pier that ringed a cove on the island's northern tip. That crescent pier was only interrupted by a short fifty-foot sandy beach section accessible by stairs. Just behind that beach sat a kayak shed. Jesper, our host, occasionally guided island guests on short kayaking trips around the neighboring islands. But when not in use, these kayaks were available for the volunteers, and Kelsy and I chose our colorful steeds at about 9 p.m. that evening.

Full-body dry suits and hoods were the often required attire for this activity. The tidal action, stiff winds, and swirling seas often combined to form a chop that both doused the unprepared kayaker and risked a quick and frigid demise if a kayak tipped over.

But that night, it seemed the entire ocean took on the persona of the tired laborer who collapsed on the couch after a hard day of work. Or perhaps it was Njǫrd (the Nordic Poseidon) that I was picturing, exhausted from the constant swells, waves, and currents that were his mythical responsibility, and taking an evening to catch his breath. Therefore, the dry suits were left behind tonight, and complete tranquility reined absolute over the canals and waterways as our kayaks' ripples first creased the water's surface. After waving to our comrades, who were lazily enjoying an evening in the wood-fired hot tub, we turned southward and slowly glided towards the prominent ridge of Måløya island in the distance.

We kept the sharp peaks of the Fjords to our left as we headed towards the three soft grassy humps that made Måløya such an easy marker. The light gurgling water around the kayaks and the occasional bump of my clumsy paddle against the side were the only sounds as we continued to slice through the water. As we slid past a beach, I could see the ocean taking deep, content breaths as the water occasionally swelled to creep up the dull gray pebbles. Then receded just as gracefully into its brilliantly turquoise domain.

The beauty of the ocean was lost on a group of birds, however, as they cried protestations against the swells that drove them from their buffet within nearby tidal pools. It was while watching these birds retreat amongst the gravel that I caught sight of a break in the, until now, constant color gradient of grey and blue from land to sea. A vivid pink spot demanded investigation perhaps ten feet offshore, and I paddled in to oblige.

After slowing as I neared my target – and a potentially embarrassing grounding on the nearby beach – I waited for the ripples from my movement to subside before observing a striking starfish. The crystal-clear water made it impossible for me to gauge its depth. Still, the vivid pink splashed another color across the turquoise canvas that the ocean provided. Widening my gaze revealed perhaps a dozen identical starfish within the immediate area, brilliant drops of pink that made me marvel at the artistry of nature.

We then glided swiftly out from this beach to continue south and occasionally stopped to admire several small sailing ships enjoying the calm evening as we were. When framed against the rugged mountains, their broad white sails seemed to create just another of the many snow-filled basins that dotted the slate-grey landscape. Another melding of sea and mountain as every boat deployed their last scrap of sail to catch the faintest whisper of wind on that calm evening.

By this time, we began to circle Måløya and the three steep hills that formed its western flank. As we coasted near shore, we kept our eyes peeled for the famous sea eagles of the region. But we instead spotted several rectangular openings in a cliff that marked the border of the first hill.

Kelsy's love of adventure was only matched by her curiosity. "Hey, we should check those out!" She called from her kayak and immediately paddled for shore without further discussion.

Well, it seemed I could drift offshore and wait for the exploration results, or I could paddle in for a little impromptu cave exploring and possible troll sighting. There was no decision-making process in my mind, and I quickly altered course to follow her kayak ahead of me.

After a precarious disembarkation, we hauled our kayaks onto the sandy beach and headed for the openings in the cliff. Upon closer inspection, we found that they weren't natural caves at all but instead had the look of artificial tunnels. Perhaps from a mining probe looking for minerals worth extracting.

Regardless of their formation, we concluded that the rock looked stable enough, drawing from vast amounts of cave experience that neither of us had, and we headed in. We soon found that internal lateral shafts connected the rectangular entrances seen from the outside, a fun discovery as we began our exploration.

A quick scramble up a steep ramp, with an assist from an old fishing rope from a previous visitor, brought us to the uppermost entrance. This rectangularly carved opening captured the snowcapped mountains on the mainland with a beautiful glass-like ocean foreground better than any painting or picture ever could.

The extreme stillness of the evening, compounded by the muffling effect of the cave, suddenly hit me. Just as diving underwater mutes the sounds of a crowded beach and commotion abruptly, I was suddenly starkly aware of the beauty and serenity of the evening and my surroundings. I imagine practiced meditators experience a similar phenomenon when the clamor of life fades to the background. Such was my experience here, where the entire world seemingly eased back, took a collective breath, and parted life's bluster and noise to create this one image. Kelsy also felt the moment's calm, and we both stayed completely still for several moments. I then voiced my displeasure at the fact that we didn't get to see one of Norway's famous trolls in this cave, and I was rebuked with an eye roll as we made our way back down to our kayaks and again pushed out to sea.

We looped around the northern edge of Måløya and now began our trip back home. Neither of us had a watch or phone accessible to judge the time, but the sun was now as low as it was going to get as it barely kissed the horizon. It could have been 11 p.m., midnight, or even 1 a.m., and the stillness seemed to increase even more as we realized all the earlier sailboats had vanished.

We were alone on an endless pane of glass, broken only by the black humps of nearby islands that were perfectly reflected in the water. The only sound was the sluice of our paddles. Even the birds had called it a day and retired for the night. The silence was so profound that both Kelsy and I stopped talking. It seemed inappropriate to break the peacefulness of the scene, just as you wouldn't speak during a beautiful violin solo at a classical music performance. We glided along in silence, admiring the reflections of mountains extending out to our bows and the gentle light of the midnight sun casting dazzling reflections across the ocean.

Suddenly, my peacefulness was silently shattered. While glancing at the tranquil water, I caught sight of a shadow that I took to be a reflection from a nearby island. That evaluation was immediately revised, however, when I registered that the dark shadow was moving directly toward my kayak from the left.

The clearness of the water allowed me to see the ocean floor beneath me, at perhaps twenty to thirty feet. Across this floor, some creature was moving closer and closer. I had stopped paddling to watch while fully dumbfounded. Seconds passed, and I wondered if this is what shark attack victims see: a dark smudge in the water gliding silently and malevolently towards them, and then nothing.

Thankfully my fears were misplaced. As the smudge swam under my kayak, giving me my first clear look, I marveled at how large a halibut could grow. I saw that the bottom-hugging flat fish easily outweighed me and could effortlessly flip my kayak if it was so inclined. After all, I was the interloper in this watery paradise, intruding where calm and silence reigned. Luckily for me, the fish went about its business and gave me time to lower my heart rate and think about our chef, Ant, who would give his right leg for a fresh halibut.

After this chance encounter, we continued our leisurely pace back to our home island. Our adventure then drew to a close as we dragged the kayaks onto our beach. While rinsing them with fresh water before heaving them into their slots in the shed, I smiled inwardly as I thought how we had glided across the ocean during one of her most serene and calming times, surrounded by the beauty of the sea and majesty of the coastal mountains. And all from an offhand idea hatched just a few hours before.

Only Antony was displeased with our evening adventure when I returned halibut-less. No fishing gear, spear, or even a net. And yet, his retort in his classical English accent still echoes through my mind when I weigh the cons of leaping into a new adventure or activity. "So what? Get after it, mate."

5

A Brief Encounter – Lofoten

The Lofoten Islands were always there. Swirling in the misty distance like the jagged spines of a giant sea serpent. Perhaps thirty miles away to the northwest and tantalizingly suspended between the horizon and vast Norwegian Sea, those dark mountain islands seemed almost mythical in their remoteness. A far-flung kingdom shrouded in mist and fortified with ancient rock that only heroes described in ancient poems ventured to for adventure and glory. I often imagined Homer's poem *The Odyssey* coming to life with Odysseus sailing off into the mists to narrowly avoid falling prey to sirens or the famous Scandinavian story of *Beowulf* unfolding as he battles with the monsters hiding in those mountains.

Our cabin's front door faced that daunting mountainous archipelago, and it quickly became part of my morning routine to stop and marvel before starting the day. As intimidating as those dark mountains appeared, I found that they offered a comforting and steadying hand on those crisp mornings. No matter how bleary-eyed I started the day as I rushed to the main kitchen to get Astrid's bread in the oven and lay out breakfast for the guests, there was something resolute about that first view. Timeless and absolute, they were a steadfast marker to orient my mind, and I repeatedly promised myself a visit there.

Luck contrived in my favor in the form of two visiting couples from eastern Europe who booked a RIB (Rigid Inflatable Boat) journey to those distant islands. Just four seats on a boat that held twenty, and Jesper wouldn't let the opportunity to show us one of Norway's more beautiful locations pass by, as he explained to our small group of volunteers.

"Only," Jesper thought critically for a moment. "The guests don't know that you haven't paid to go on the boat, so don't tell them."

An unmistakably conspiratorial grin jumped from me to Jonas, Ola, Kelsy, and Jesper. "Deal," I agreed for all of us. I wasn't about to turn down an adventure to Lofoten, especially when it appeared to be on an unknowing benefactor's dime.

Our preparations for an overpowered speed boat trip to Lofoten continued to mirror the seemingly perilous journey to that jagged and daunting land. Layers upon layers of waterproof gear flowed out of the boat's forward hatch, followed by neon yellow life preservers.

Our captain carefully handed these items to every passenger, "If you go in the water with no protection, you have only six minutes." Our benefactors' grasp of English appeared to be slight. Yet their female companions seemed to understand this warning and noticeably clenched their life jackets while darting pleading looks at the two men.

The last items passed around were clear safety glasses – an accessory I'd never thought I'd be required to wear on a boat trip. Our captain explained it succinctly enough, "we go very fast," he stated while pointing to the distant spine of mountains and then to the pair of comically massive engines perched on the back of the long, slender craft. "If very fast salt water hit your eye, it hurts."

I briefly thought about how a speeding drop of icy salt water slamming into my eyeball at sixty miles per hour would feel. I blinked away the perceived pain and quickly slipped on my safety glasses. My imagination of Odysseus crossing an unknown sea was sufficient without a poor imitation of the Cyclops joining the adventure.

Those thirty miles seemed to melt away ahead of the mighty roar of the overpowered RIB boat. Every glance back toward the mountains seemed to bring them noticeably closer.

The contours and textures of those distinctive mountain faces slowly came into focus. Each seemed dark and foreboding, like the weathered Jötnar giants of Norse mythology with their icy, snow-bound heads. Each spectacularly sharp peak, chiseled shoulder, and vast cliff plunging straight into the sea gave this ice-carved land a character of its own.

I marveled and imagined how any town or city could find space to coexist with these broad giants. Even at that rapidly diminishing distance, every scrap of rocky land seemed part of an impossibly steep mountain. And yet, I was told that a string of villages existed here, and we were heading to one called Henningsvær.

A dark shape floating in front of the mountains slowly took shape as the famous Hurtigruten ferry and our captain's focused face split into a wide grin. I noticed him shift his weight and lean noticeably to his right, and I only had time to briefly wonder if the view was really much better over there before he violently spun the wheel. Momentum almost flung the rest of us from our seats as we desperately grabbed handrails and each other to keep from careening off into the ocean. We seemed suspended over oblivion for a split second as the boat lurched through its hard right turn.

We had cut towards the massive, lumbering ferry. I heard a sharp hoot of joy as the captain pushed the throttle to the stop and aimed for the ferry's rolling wake, mixed with a sharp scream of terror from the front of the boat as one of our guests realized what was about to happen. We only had time to clutch our metal-framed seats before the boat catapulted over the wave and became entirely airborne momentarily. One of the men up front raised his hands like he was on a rollercoaster before we crashed back into the ocean, jolting us all once more. Our white knuckles slowly relaxed as the captain eased the throttles and lazily steered us to a collection of buildings that materialized from behind the ferry's plump shape.

I was captivated by the village that opened up before us. Packed onto small strips of land sitting delicately in the shadow of one of Lofoten's prominent mountains, the robustly squat buildings seemed to be clinging to whatever flat land they could find. But as I quickly learned, flat land always ran short in Lofoten. Here in Henningsvær, generations of hardy locals had turned a waterway between two long spits of land into their main thoroughfare with sturdy wooden and concrete docks lining its entire length to make room for even more buildings cantilevered over the Norwegian Sea.

But what grabbed my attention most was the warm color. Striking red and bright mustard yellow facades dappled those streets in sharp contrast to the dark greys of the stone giant looming above. Bright signs called out *fersk fisk* and *varm mat* as vibrant cafes touted their deliciously fresh fish and hot meals in stout defiance of the bitter sea and unforgiving mountains that flanked them on all sides.

One such café caught our attention with a broad wooden deck protruding over the turquoise water. Without the typical scattered clouds threatening their usual fifteen-minute rain showers, the water shimmered brilliantly in the uninterrupted sun as it delicately splashed on the soft algae-covered rocks below. But the true draw for our little group was the massive bowl of fish stew and fresh bread that had just been served to another patron seated on the deck. The blustery and chilly speedboat crossing still showed brightly on our flushed cheeks, and we didn't bother wasting breath on words as we agreed that this establishment was for us.

Jesper spotted the steaming bowl of fish stew first and turned to the rest of us. Both bushy black eyebrows shot up and he tilted his head towards the unknowing patron who barely had time to lift his spoon before we were scrutinizing his meal from the street. Once Jesper was sure we were looking in the right direction, his eyebrows ticked up another notch while his beard parted into a smile.

I simply winked while Kelsy let out a laugh and started walking to the café door without bothering to look at the rest of our group. She knew very well that we were heading in.

Jonas also smiled broadly and gave his stomach a very audible slap – enough to draw the other café patron's attention and a bewildered expression. Then, just a few minutes later, we were also seated on the deck with our own bowls of stew and what seemed like an entire loaf of bread divided among our plates.

Between soul-warming bites of buttery cod and potato soup, I took the opportunity to admire this remarkable village. Our deck was perched above the main waterway bisecting the town, and we watched the steady march of local fishermen, vacation boats, and larger tourist charters filter through this ocean boulevard.

I'd never seen a place so intimately connected to the sea before. While there was one solitary road leap-frogging from the mainland across not one but two small islands via an intricate bridge network, it was clear that the sea was this area's true connection to the world. What little rocky shoreline that wasn't occupied by a building hosted a series of matchstick-like structures that I soon learned were old-fashioned fish drying racks. While most of them were simply for aesthetics to highlight the area's fishing history – as I learned from Jesper – the constant screech of gulls near a few of the racks was clear evidence that at least a few were still in use.

However, I was still just as entranced by the mountains here as I was thirty miles away on our front porch back home. Their sharp peaks surged thousands of feet into the air while rocky cliffs plunged straight into the ocean to form the bedrock that held this fantastical place together. Looking to the right and left, the mountains unfolded all the way to the horizon, an endless maze of rugged beauty. Behind us, the closest mountains seemed built on layers, each competing for the best position by shoving each other aside and thrusting their competitive peaks higher and higher to see which one would win – creating a mosaic of mountains that I could just barely make out a distant hiking trail disappearing into its intricate design.

With this mountainous backdrop, the village seemed to be a living entity comfortably hunkered into what seemed like one of the most beautifully harsh places in the world. After our hearty fish stew, friendly lights beckoned up and down the streets as we explored, waving us into every shop or market like a well-meaning local. Meanwhile, the steady water lazily wafting through that center canal made the village appear to be breathing deep, tranquil sighs. The fulfilling exhales of one who was content, and that was simply enough.

Our allotted afternoon there expired too soon with a shrill whistle from our captain about fifty yards up the main channel at the public dock. But as we made that last walk through the stone-flagged streets, I smiled back at the friendly world that had allowed me to visit. I left that village with the same emotions as I would leave a dear friend. Heavy-hearted to return to my own life separate from theirs, but fulfilled to have this friendship on the other side of the world. A friendship that I've rekindled in the years since that first trip, and forever grateful for the resonating connection that a fleeting visit created.

6

Boots, Backpacks, and a New Life

I believe Jesper took extreme pleasure and pride in breaking a city-slicker to the Arctic island way of life. His large Viking face always cracked into a wide grin whenever he saw me toiling in the muck, chasing sheep, or giving the wooden hot tub its regular scrape down. But no matter my exhaustion level, I always grinned back; because I was having the time of my life.

That island work took me to every corner of the hospitality business. From assisting Jesper's partner Astrid prepare breakfast for guests in the morning to helping clean cabins after they departed, I saw and did it all. And strangely, hospitality did not immediately return me to my engineering career. After all, the well-regimented corporate life rarely saw me cleaning up after others or hustling to prepare the perfect Norwegian breakfast in the morning – so why wouldn't I chalk this island trip down to life experience and head back to my well-ordered life?

Novelty, of course, played a role. Here was something I'd never attempted before, and the exhilaration of exploring a new place and trying new tasks was significant. And yet, there was something else that I felt almost immediately. There was a strange thrill in meeting new people and facilitating their happiness that was instantly and strangely addictive. Every morning brought new faces and stories, while every task was immediately beneficial and appreciated. Meanwhile, every off moment could be spent exploring new mountains and islands that each seemed like an ideal locale for the trolls and fairies of Norwegian legend. Jesper had already changed the course of my life by showing me this world. But now he was about to personally usher me into a new career that would blend every aspect of what I loved about travel into a single job – guiding.

I started that morning utterly unaware of the turn signal approaching my life. It was a typically overcast morning with billowing waves of clouds breaking against the mountains – a gargantuan parody of the soft morning waves on the pier – before tumbling down their rocky sides into the valleys below. The snow had recently receded from the top of the nearby mountains on the mainland, and patches of vivid green materialized in those upper reaches to mark the beginning of summer. My typical morning task in those days was to wake early and head to the main building to lay out breakfast for the island's guests. But this time, Jesper was waiting for me in the kitchen.

"I'm leading a group up into the mountains today," he began without preface. I noted that he was strangely out of his island caretaker uniform of a hardy-knit grey sweater and hard-worn work pants that morning. Dark brown expedition pants complemented a technical-looking fleece that immediately transformed him from a grizzled self-sufficient Nordic islander to an adventure-ready explorer preparing to take on the mountains.

"You should come too, learn the route, and then you can guide guests so I don't have to spend so much time away from the lodge." In hindsight, I realized there was never a single question in this interchange, and he knew he didn't need one.

I nodded emphatically, both envious and intimated by the amount of experience and confidence that poured out of his demeanor and clothing. I was an amateur rock climber and junior member of a search and rescue team back in Minnesota, but at that moment, I knew that I had everything in the world to learn about the outdoors, and Jesper was ready to teach. No question needed; I knew I was going.

The mountain in question was Sørskottinden. Towering above the small village of Nordskot, this mountain formed the southern watchtower of the massive rock wall that shielded Nordskot from the rest of Norway – the Nordskot Traverse. The traverse was a half-mile-long rock wall that heaved straight out of the soft mossy forest to form a jagged barrier hundreds of feet high on either side and only a few feet wide at its narrowest point. At the northern end of this intimidating fixture was yet another mountain, completing a giant's castle with the soft turquoise hues of the ocean in sharp contrast to the vast towers of gray rock and occasional snow patch that shielded it from the rest of the world.

That snowy rock barrier exuded an aura of impenetrability, allowing nothing to pass from the picturesque rural houses of the village at its base to the outside world. But that was precisely what we were going to do – myself, Jesper, and three additional visitors to the island – and what I would do regularly in the coming months.

The expedition began with a short boat ride, followed by an equally succinct drive to the trailhead. Astrid promised to meet our team at the other end of our journey, and her comfortable-looking jeep disappeared into the morning fog all too quickly. Now it was just the deep greens of the ancient forest and our team.

Jesper's face crinkled into a smile as he presented me with a tightly wrapped, sixty-meter climbing rope. As he put it, the "honor" of carrying the rope was mine since it was my training hike.

"More like here's another ten pounds you don't want to carry up there," I scoffed while gesturing vaguely to the swirling mists that revealed only occasional glimpses of the stone massif in front of us.

"I don't know what pounds are," Jesper deflected with a wink. "Here, coil it up like this and sling it over your shoulder for the hike," he continued as he heaved the rope over my head and shoulder and nodded approvingly like a parent sending their child to school for the first time.

That served as a signal to our group, and packs met backs as everyone shouldered their bags and appraised the adventure they'd decided to join. I could see from the stoned-faced determination carved into my group's faces that they, too, were feeling the full weight of their decision to join this hike. The clouds mockingly parted just at that moment, and we were now looking the eight-hundred-meter climb to the summit of Sørskottinden full in the face. The unexpected climbing rope slung over my shoulders made me feel like an interloper preparing to scale the walls of some colossal castle. With that last fleeting thought, Jesper plunged into the forest, and we all filed into a line to follow.

Within five minutes of hitting the trail, we started a steep ascent that would remain painfully constant for the next two hours until we hit the top. We climbed and climbed and climbed as the trail meandered between densely packed trees and boggy clearings. The occasional bubbling creek crossing added a couple of long jumps to our day of track and field activity. But with every curve in the trail, I expected to finally catch a glimpse of our summit destination, only to see more trees rising up into the mist like a mocking peanut gallery filling an amphitheater to infinity.

There didn't look like this much forest from the outside. I thought as I unzipped my fleece layer to keep from overheating and swiftly added, *said every person who's ever gotten lost.* This potential epitaph gave me a smile, and I took the time to appreciate the ancient arctic forest we were exploring.

We were bounded by the deep greens of numerous pines, spruces, and birches that worked in tandem with the lighter greens from thick tufts of ground moss to paint a soothing pallet of color against the stark grey rock outcroppings that we observed with ever-increasing frequency. Swirling wisps of grey mist from the approaching cloud front soon added to the enchanted sensation as we were enveloped by the mist in a mysterious and ominous world. Then, just as the massive freighters on Lake Superior would emerge from the fog back home as a ghostly shade, the bare face of rock would thrust itself back into view as if the mountain itself was checking on our progress. Trees would drift by, disconnected and disembodied, singly bobbing past in the mist with no earthly connection as they marked our progress like lonely buoys at sea.

While an intriguing and engaging atmosphere, which kept our group plowing forward without the slightest hint of tiring, the doubt I felt earlier grew more intense as I thought of potentially rappelling and scrambling on top of massive cliffs when every surface was wet from this mist. Nonetheless, Jesper seemed entirely unfazed and confident as he led us forward. He'd occasionally turn back with a smile to check our progress or call out a friendly snippet of encouragement.

But just once, after turning back to the trail from checking on our group, I caught him running his hand over a rock outcropping. Shimmering black with moisture, I saw Jesper rub the dampness between his calloused fingers as he contemplated the dangers of climbing in such conditions, and his expression clouded to match the skies. He caught me observing him, and his two dark bushy eyebrows rose together like a mini pair of shrugging shoulders. Then, just as quickly, the lines on his face softened, and the friendly eye crinkles returned as he pivoted back to our group with another smiling round of encouragement.

Message received. We'd see when we got there. No use worrying the group until we knew what mighty Sørskottinden had in store for us. Perhaps one of the most vital lessons of my fledging career, and there wasn't a word spoken.

After another twenty minutes of pushing upward, we finally caught sight of a ledge looming above us, black with moisture and devoid of any trees beyond. A beacon from the mountain, saying that we were breaking from the forest and finally getting to the 'mountaineering' aspect of our trip. Almost simultaneously, I spotted the first shadow of the day. The sun, which had until now remained completely obscured, revealed itself as a hazy pale ball hovering in the clouds above us. Better than nothing.

The trail left the dirt and mud behind, replacing it with endless rocky gravel that again hinted we were approaching the mountain's stony top. Up we scrambled, and I told myself that the clouds *must* be clearing with each step. Indeed, I was getting warmer and warmer as my shirt felt damp under the combined weight of pack and rope, but was this simply the consequence of our hike? We finally reached the top of the rocky beacon which had first hinted that we were approaching the top, and I heard a prolonged, deep sigh escape Jesper's black beard. At first, I couldn't see the reason for the sigh. He was simply looking at the slate grey top of the rocky ledge we had observed from below. Jesper smiled and scrapped his boot against it, then the realization cleared the fog from my head just as the sun burned through the mist above us. The rock was grey, not the shiny black that we had nervously eyed up to this point. Grey, dry, grippy, and ready for us to take on the traverse.

Those last few minutes to the top of Sørskottinden revealed the first tiny fragments of the world around us. Hazy openings drifted through the clouds capturing the vibrant blues and greens of the surrounding fjords that our greyscale hike had all but erased from memory until now. One such drifting portal panned across the offshore islands, and we could just make out shimmering golden rays of sun dancing across the receding tides before our cloud bank once again closed ranks.

As we continued past the summit, the trail began to narrow, speaking volumes to the lessoned foot traffic that ventured this far. Our path took us down slightly, and my legs voiced their approval as we moved onto Sørskottinden's grassy eastern shoulder. Here, Jesper called a short break while he plowed ahead to check rock conditions.

Our group was relatively spaced out at this point. Giving each adventurer ample room to maneuver and hike at their own pace. I took advantage of this freedom as I plopped down on a particularly cushy tuft of tall grass and pushed a finger into each boot to confirm their water resistance had held up to that point.

At that moment, the world threw back the curtain to reveal her dazzling masterpiece. What had previously been a solid wall of grey was now Leines Fjord. At my feet, the tall clumps of hardy grass fanned downward and coalesced into a stunningly lush field punctuated by vivid red barns – the type of white-trimmed barns that evoke nostalgia and contentment even in those who have never seen them. They're simply meant to be there, keeping watch over their accompanying fields with dignified beauty. These fields then melded into the icy turquoise waters of the fjord, which pushed their way forward until another series of snow-capped mountains blocked their path, funneling the sea inland towards the large town of Leinesfjord that was a barely perceptible white haze of houses in the distance.

I thought about the cramped confines of the office that had been my life and the off-grey cubical that had once been mine for eight hours a day, five days a week. The safe career was there, along with a plethora of items that I was told I wanted. Yet, Sørskottinden and luck had just thrown back the veil on what I needed, and it was so simple. It was right there. The mountains, the calm, the ocean, and the adventure. I laughed at that moment, knowing that I had just made a monumental decision, and yet the most life-altering decisions are the easiest when you know what you want. *This is going to be my office*, I thought, *this is going to be my life, and **that** beautiful fellow can make it happen.*

Jesper had returned from his scout and beckoned me with an outstretched finger. I trotted over to him like a pup admiring the grizzled pack leader. I have no doubt that he knew the series of thoughts that had cascaded through my mind. However, like most Norwegians, Jesper wasn't one for emotional conversations about such trifles as life's wants and directions. But he knew and simply gave me a wink and a dry "It's a nice view, isn't it?"

I breathlessly agreed and stayed on his heels as he took me to my first look at the Nordskot Traverse. We now stood above that rocky bridge that connected us to the next mountain. Indeed, the traverse looked like Sørskottinden had flung an arm around the adjacent mountain's shoulder, and the two were now locked in a perpetual bond that we were fixing to cross. The entire length of the traverse was a rocky palisade, bounded by a two-hundred-foot drop-off on either side that led straight back into the steep mountainous forest from which we had just emerged.

While most of the traverse was a straightforward hike with a dash of scrambling, it started as a single twenty-foot ledge dropping from our current position on Sørskottinden's shoulder down to the traverse itself. For this section, Jesper showed me how to set up a rappel. I finally unslung the rope I'd lugged since our day started and followed Jesper's every move as he explained the anchors, procedure, and safety. I was no stranger to rock climbing or the hardware, but the thought of ushering a large group safely through this maneuver sharpened my attention.

"Here, you try it," Jesper instructed as he handed me two anchors to wedge into a distinct crack in the rock.

I fumbled with the anchors like they were two squirming creatures instead of the familiar hardware I'd handled a hundred times before. My nervousness at being observed by such a professional – and three additional pairs of onlooking eyes – oozed through my every action.

I worked through my incompetent dexterity as I finally opened the proper filing cabinet in my head for rock climbing, and the anchors slipped into place with a satisfied grunt from Jesper. From there, he and I at last made use of that cumbersome rope and anchored it to the rock. Guests who were experienced could rappel themselves down to the waiting ledge. For those that weren't, we lowered through a simple pulley tool. Once it was just me and Jesper left at the top, we removed the anchors, wrapped the rope around a conical rock,

DANIEL PURDY

and rappelled down one at a time using the rock as an anchor. At the bottom, we simply pulled on one end of the rope and slipped it out from around the rock, where it then fell into a pile at our feet. No going back now.

After we reassembled at the bottom of the rappel, Jesper offered another lesson as he demonstrated tying butterfly knots at about thirty-foot increments in the rope. The guests and I watched in rapt attention, imagining our fates woven into those knots as Jesper explained the principles of rope team hiking. We'd all connect our harnesses to those knots and hike spaced out enough to leave just a little slack between each person. Therefore, if someone took a wrong step and fell, the rest of our party only had to drop to the ground, and the immense friction of sixty meters of rope on rock would keep the unlucky hiker from plummeting off the side of the Traverse. A fine tactic when discussed from safety; I hoped we wouldn't have to put it to the test that day.

The going was cautiously easy as we carefully chose our footing or opted for the occasional butt-slide to safely navigate the rocks and keep a safe distance between us and the edge. In fact, the endless panorama of fjords enraptured our attention and made the traverse seem to fly by. But as we neared the end, where it once again rejoined the mountains, I noticed the edges of the traverse narrowing sharply into a distinct flat-topped rock.

Probably just an illusion, I told myself, and we continued to pick our way forward. *There must be an easy path around that.*

Several minutes passed, and I occupied my thoughts with how Jesper would expertly find a hidden path to take us around the obstacle. An observer to a magic trick, I held my breath for the magnificent finale when our group came to a stop just as the traverse began to bottleneck to this single point. Instead, Jesper turned to me and again signaled me forward with his telling smile.

Damn, I thought as I shuffled to join him. *No way around after all.*

"I call this the 'hugging rock,'" Jesper said through his smile. "This is where everyone needs the most help."

"Not surprising," I replied dryly, studying the obstacle before us. "Help from not dying, I suppose."

The 'hugging rock', as I also called it after that, was more of a stone pillar cleanly sheared off at about ten feet. It measured only about three feet wide at the top and funneled the climber onto a stony spine with sheer drop-offs on either side before the traverse finally opened up again onto the next mountain's shoulder.

While the rest of our rope team maintained their distance and proper rope tension, Jesper showed me how it was done. His instructions were precise, right down to where feet and hands needed to be as he lifted himself partway up the pillar. Then, in one fluid motion, he heaved himself up and onto the rock, scrambled his way across the stone spine with surprising nimbleness for such a tall man, and turned to observe my rendering of his instructions.

"Okay, foot here," I said aloud as I tried to replicate Jesper's smoothness. "Right foot... somewhere..." my foot scrambled and scraped against the rock as I fought to find the proper placement, "right there." I threw my left arm over the top of the pillar onto its almost flat surface, desperately working my fingers into every mossy crevice, trying to find the correct hold.

"No, nope!" Jesper called for his safe perch on stable ground. "A little more to the left... left!"

I followed his instructions as I flailed my arm further out to the side of the rock and leaned in to find the correct hold. "There!" I finally had a good grip, and the rock's name was suddenly brought into sharp relief. I was clinging to the side of a stone pillar, both feet tucked into subtle pockets as my body hung precariously over an incredibly scenic yet equally catastrophic plummet into the fjord below me. The only way around that fate was to give this lousy rock the biggest bear hug possible and shimmy my way upwards to get up and over.

"Stop right there!" Jesper called. He was clearly waiting for this exact moment. When the realization of the height, exposure, and awkwardness hit me, my eyes no doubt telegraphed those feelings better than any words. "This is exactly how all your guests will feel," he continued. "Think about how to coax them through it."

"I'm trying to get myself through it first!" I called half-jokingly, half pleading for quiet as I calmed my racing thoughts and focused on the problem at hand. Foot up, hand creeping forward, a firm push, a whispered expletive, and I was suddenly standing on that hugging rock. The entire Nordskot Traverse and fjord sprawled dramatically behind me, almost too close for comfort as one half-step back would permanently add me to the landscape.

I quickly scooted forward, Jesper continued ahead to maintain our rope tension, and the guest behind me now had to conquer the same obstacle.

"You're up," Jesper said, echoing the voice in my head as I turned back to offer moral support for the herculean effort unfolding behind me. This particular guest was nearly a foot shorter than I, and her disadvantage in reach made the heart-pounding climb over the hugging rock a much more prolonged ordeal.

But she made up for what she lacked in height with gusto as she took on a look of stone-faced determination. She hurled herself at the first set of directions I offered. But that resolve seemed to melt as she hugged the rock, realizing she didn't know what to do next but was fully committed to moving forward since backtracking involved looking down.

I summoned the confidence I'd seen Jesper project earlier and called out advice. "Your left foot to that shelf on your left." She stared at me blankly for a moment before wiggling her right foot. "Your left!" I called again.

She finally responded, although it sounded more like an exploding gasp that she tried to form into words as an afterthought. "I ... ah ... I am afraid of heights!"

This was the first I'd heard of this malady during the entire hike. I couldn't move to her to assist as that would defeat the purpose of our rope, nor could the person behind her move forward to help.

I took a deep breath. "Stop for a second and look at me!" This time she complied immediately. "Look, I've got you," I held up the rope snaking through my harness to emphasize the point. "You're not going anywhere. Just breathe, and pull with your left hand. It's just like a ladder, only it's hiding."

She laughed at my poor humor attempt, but it had the desired effect. With a warrior howl, she scaled the rock and pulled herself to a standing position in one fluid motion. She first stood there like a deer in the headlights, wide-eyed, arms held cautiously out to the sides like something might push her over, and seemingly checking in with her body to make sure everything had made the climb.

"You did it!" I called to help her brain realize the hard part was behind her.

She looked straight into my eyes and soul. First in shock, and I feared she might teeter back over the edge. Then a smile slowly started forming at a dimple on her left cheek. It creased downward to her lip and then arced back to her right cheek to form such a massive grin that I never thought possible from such a little woman. Her hands shot straight upward, and she screamed in triumph.

I barely knew this woman. We had only met that morning and talked intermittently during the day. Yet at that moment, I cared for her success as if we were the best of friends in the world. And for an instant, we were. I raised my arms in celebration before snatching my phone and capturing a quick picture of her moment on top of the world. She was my first guest as a guide, and her triumph and accomplishment still make me smile whenever I remember that moment.

I looked back at Jesper as we began to move forward again. I was still flush with exhilaration from that triumph, and his usual laconic response was a simple wink. It was enough, and I grinned broadly again. *I could love this job,* I thought, as we slowly began our descent.

7

Wild Man

I admired Børge Ousland immensely. Yet, we never chatted or asked how one another's day was going or even spent more than an hour or so in each other's presence during my three months in Norway.

The owner of that little island lodge was rarely there. But whenever he appeared, it was with yards of PVC pipe in hand, a bucket of hardware, or whatever other supplies he brought on the ferry to continue his slow but steady creation of Manshausen.

Børge's presence on the island was, therefore, often marked by an early wake-up call from the high-pitched whine of a wood saw as he built a sauna and walkway plank by plank. The accompanying staccato of hammer blows would continue to echo throughout the island until well after dinner. The man seemed to work from sunrise to sunset, which proved doubly impressive in a land where the sun never set at all.

Indeed, he seemed to be a man of extreme focus, seeing what projects needed to be done or obstacles to be overcome with shocking clarity. Whether that solemn resolve came before or after his service in the Norwegian Special Forces, I couldn't say. Or before or after his time as a deep-sea diver in the North Sea. Or perhaps after he became one of the first people to reach the North Pole unsupported. Or the first person ever to cross all of Antarctica solo and unaided.

But that resolve showed in his eyes. They were dark and weathered with the perpetual seriousness of a man accustomed to working hard. I could easily picture those same eyes crinkled with equal concentration as Børge measured a wooden step to perfection or stared into the face of a polar bear on the frozen arctic tundra.

But his exceptionally lanky six-foot frame didn't exactly represent the extreme adventurer that he was.

Børge wasn't the massively burly explorer that we often picture. But his razor-sharp cheekbones, slightly padded by an ever-present grey scruff, tightly set mouth that always lingered halfway between a faint smile and scowl, and those severe eyes all spoke to a man not to be trifled with.

Not that Børge spoke of his background to us – least of all to me. He was classically Norwegian in that sense. He seemed to bristle at the slightest hint of small talk yet readily discussed maintenance projects on the island or any other subject that required his attention. But any superfluous conversation was clearly encroaching on the voluminous personal bubble that many Norwegians seemed to carry with them. Never rude, never standoffish, simply kept to themselves, and that was Børge, as far as I could tell.

Yet a dash of curiosity about our lodge's stoic owner seasoned with a pinch of hearsay as Jesper alluded to his "past expeditions" was all I needed to justify spending a few megabytes of our cabin's coveted internet data. As the full resume scrolled in front of my eyes, my slight intimidation morphed into admiration.

At the time, I was still in the honeymoon phase of my newfound love of the outdoors and adventure. Therefore, whenever Børge materialized on the island, it was as if the king of the outdoors himself had arrived, and I was consequently embarrassingly, blubberingly, and hopelessly awkward.

So instead of having a productive conversation about building my skills or experience, I took on the role of an enamored observer. I was acutely aware whenever Børge was in the vicinity and tried to learn about what makes such a successful outdoor adventurer through surreptitious scrutinizing while trying to nonchalantly complete my tasks. It makes no sense, and it didn't then, but *c'est la vie* – that's the result of the stereotypical social ineptitude that my engineering path left me.

It was during one of these observances I spotted Børge finally taking some time off for himself, which alone seemed a miracle due to his never-ending workload. As I replaced the fraying ropes holding our boat's rubber bumpers in place, I saw him heading down to the rocky shore. Now, I'd expect time off for such a busy man to look like a comfortable book on the couch or even a nap – he'd certainly earned it – but the adventurous spirit of a man like that never seems to ebb.

He was clad in a pitch-black wetsuit from hooded head to foot. The low steely grey clouds and jagged coastal rocks added even more solemnity to the picture as this darkly dressed man with dark eyes slowly trudged toward the icy water. But most eye-catching, however, was the four-foot-long spear gun slung over his shoulder – also black. Børge either didn't see me observing him or didn't care, and I'm inclined to believe the latter as he reached the water's edge, propped his spear gun onto a rock, and made a few final adjustments to his hood.

Jonas now joined me, his regular comedic grin showing as he was about to say something frivolous. But his eyes followed mine to the beach, and even Jonas became a serious observer of Børge's preparations, a change of attitude that was almost unprecedented for Jonas.

We both knew how frigid those waters were, hanging in the upper forties Fahrenheit. Cold enough to deliver fatal hypothermia shockingly fast.

"At least he has a wetsuit," Jonas offered as Børge secured the last Velcro strap holding his hood in place, and pulled on his thick gloves.

Wetsuit be dammed. I thought to myself. Reinforcing the fact that slipping into the Norwegian Sea wasn't my idea of relaxing during time off. "What's he fishing for?"

"He said halibut earlier," Jonas replied without taking his eyes off the final preparations before us.

But I swiveled towards him, my eyebrows crinkled in consternation as I grappled with this new information. "Aren't those three hundred pounds?" I asked, breathlessly shocked that a man who looked to weigh about one hundred eighty pounds in a soaking-wet wetsuit would actively seek out such a giant underwater.

"I think so," Jonas replied as he closed his blue eyes to focus on math. "they could be around one-hundred-sixty kilos; I think that's closer to four hundred pounds."

I turned around again to watch Børge begin to wade into the water, his black wetsuit immediately becoming invisible in the dark water with each step. *Holy shit, that's one wild man.*

We continued watching the water for a few moments longer, and just barely perceived a black snorkel break the surface before disappearing. Then he was gone, seemingly invisible to everything both above and below the surface of the water as he stealthily looked for that massive fish. And fittingly, I found that stealthy approach fitting for this man.

He was the sole reason that any of us ended up on that island. Manshausen was his dream and creation, and without him, I'd never have had the opportunity to have any of these experiences. Yet, Børge seemed to excel at keeping a low profile when he was on the island. He'd very subtly and unobtrusively move into his room in the volunteer house – **his** house – such that we'd sometimes never even know he was on the island until we heard him working the next morning.

He seemed to be the type that led from the back. If there was an unpleasant job to do, he wouldn't hesitate to pick up a shovel and jump into the mud with us. He'd help direct our efforts, most definitely; but his instructions always seemed to come across as friendly suggestions such that we almost forgot he was the boss at all. In fact, I'd never have known that the sinewy man toiling on the wooden footpath was even Børge and the owner of this place if Jesper hadn't told me.

It's taken me several years of growth and navigating life to realize what an important trait this is, and, over the course of revisiting these memories, to realize that although I never substantially spoke with him, I still came away with a valuable lesson. To help others experience the same magic that travel and adventure offer, I can't be the backcountry boss dictating what to enjoy, appreciate, and do. I'm right there with them, the friend at their side who's invested in their triumph while getting just as dirty as we work together, and my reward is watching them fall in love with the world again.

8

Exploring the Darkness

There's something in the water in those upper reaches of coastal Norway. A particular mixture that yields the most hardy and extraordinary yet friendly and humble people I've ever encountered. A perfect example was Randi, our next-door neighbor, during my time in Nordskot.

Of course, in this sense, "next door" meant climbing into our hardy Hansuik work boat, puttering about fifty yards to the adjacent island, and walking up to the distinctive two-story white cabin and matching barn. But the journey was always worth it to spend some time with Randi.

I couldn't guess her age when we first met – after being loaned by Jesper to help her move some rubbish the tide had left behind. Perhaps in her late fifties, I'd have guessed, owing to her short snowy-white hair and the endearing crinkles around her eyes when she first smiled at me. But those were the only indicators of her true age, as her energy and strength immediately blew me away so fast that I risked whiplash.

Jonas and I arrived at Randi's doorstep mid-morning on a surprisingly brisk yet sunny June day. Although we had never met before, Randi threw open her door and pulled us into the kitchen area for a hot drink with that instant friendliness and welcoming spirit that I loved so much about that part of the world. After a steaming cup of tea and exchanging introductions with her and her cat, she pulled on her rubber boots and simple green wool beanie, and we got to work.

Randi navigated the treacherously rocky shoreline of her island with shocking grace – a testament to her fitness and familiarity with the area – while Jonas and I half ran half stumbled after her to keep up. During a particularly clumsy stumble on my part, Jonas caught the disbelieving look in my eye as I watched Randi charging ahead in front of us.

"Don't worry, she's more fit than either of us will ever be."

"Clearly," was the only half-hearted response I could conjure on the spur of the moment.

"She was the first woman to summit Everest, you know."

This grabbed my attention. I had just taken my first steps into guiding mountain hikes and couldn't believe I was collecting rubbish with someone of legendary status in that world.

"First *Norwegian* woman to climb Everest," Jonas amended when he saw my eyes widen.

But it didn't matter. Randi's status had just jumped to the front of the line in my mind. That time in Norway had already extraordinarily reshuffled my life priorities, most notably rewiring my ambitions and goals from engineering to the great outdoors. I glanced across the choppy water to our island and remembered our lodge owner, Børge Ousland, who also held multiple records in outdoor escapades. Jonas seemed to sense my thoughts, and I didn't need to tell him who I was thinking about when I asked in all seriousness, "What is it with this place?"

He simply smiled and shrugged. We seemed surrounded by extraordinary people; all we could do was pick up the pace as Randi called for us to catch up.

But Randi's effect on my time in Norway was about to expand well beyond inspiring me to continue chasing the outdoors. Presently, our rubbish collection team came upon a large green gas cylinder. At about four feet tall with a onefoot radius, it had the look of a massive oxygen tank from a hospital. With equal parts peeling paint and rust – which had conveniently turned the label to dust many years ago – it was impossible to gauge what it contained. A trip to the recycling and reclamation center on the mainland was called for.

Both grunting and laughing at the awkwardness of the task, Jonas and I hauled the cylinder to our work boat, and all three of us piled in for the field trip to the mainland. Randi's car at the pier in Nordskot was the next leg as we drove to a recycling center near Engeløya – a glistening green island bursting with spring color connected via bridge to the rest of Norway.

The deposit at the waste center itself wasn't extraordinary, but what happened on the way back was. As we drove along a beautiful coastal road, Jonas and Randi lapsed into a brief conversation in Norwegian – or perhaps Jonas's native Danish. I didn't pay much attention as I watched stunning fields of yellow flowers extend directly to the turquoise water's edge to create another shocking canvas of color that I hardly expected to encounter in Arctic Norway.

Randi and Jonas's conversation concluded with several gestures towards a dark smudge on the coastline coming up on our right. Randi took the next turn onto a dirt road leading to the smudge – now taking shape as an ugly concrete building – as Jonas turned in his seat to tell me that this was an old Nazi bunker from the Second World War, and Randi wanted to give us a chance to see it while we were there. I nodded enthusiastically. After all, I'd always loved history, and my brief time with Randi had already convinced me that if she thought something was worth visiting, it definitely was.

But after we parked and began walking toward the old, squat concrete building recessed into a rocky hill on the coast, my first thought was *unimpressive*. Just a tiny bunker by the looks of it, with the drab yet functional concrete build of wartime. But as soon as we reached the single entrance, I revised my assessment as a slew of adjectives ran through my mind.

The entrance was a slim rectangular opening cut into several feet of concrete, revealing a set of stairs that headed straight down into darkness. Ominous, cold, menacing, melancholy, the list went downward with our feet as we took our first steps into that dark history.

That first staircase took us perhaps thirty feet underground. What started as just a bunker tucked into a hillside expanded to seemingly become an underground city, partially reclaimed by the ocean as an icy few inches of water swirled down the hallway.

The color and vibrance I loved so much about northern Norway were wrestled aside to create a black world of concrete and cold. The waves' splash and birds' chirp were abruptly muted and replaced with our tentative footsteps that reverberated up and down the passageway. Barracks, offices, mess, radio room, and countless other barren concrete chambers floated out of the darkness, only illuminated by our phone lights. We barely spoke, yet every gust of damp and chilled air flowing through this underground city seemed like a soft, collective sigh from the thousands of prisoners forced to build this place – and the hundreds that never left.

However, the German soldiers that once occupied this structure weren't simply a garrison but also caretakers for one of the most terrifying weapons of World War Two. Our wanderings through the underground bunker slowly illuminated as we approved another entrance at the back of the structure facing the sea. At this point, Randi said over her shoulder that the Germans were here to control all the shipping in the North Sea, and this was how they did it.

This rear entrance led to a concrete courtyard encircling a massive concrete pedestal festooned with dark orange hardware scraps as the salty, corrosive air reclaimed the metal components. The central pedestal was perhaps twenty feet wide, and the surrounding concrete courtyard formed concentric circles where each level rose about ten feet with each ring such that the pedestal was at the center of several concrete circular terraces, forming an arena of sorts.

The shape and scale of what I was looking at didn't immediately click. I looked at Jonas, but he was lost in thought looking at this shape, with one of the more severe expressions I'd seen on his usually grinning face. I then looked questionably to Randi, and she explained what we were looking at.

"It was a gun," she said, throwing her arms above her head to emphasize its massiveness. "Look out there," she continued, pointing to the now-visible ocean.

I obliged. It was a crisp and clear day, and the Lofoten islands were visible in the distance. Between where we stood and those islands sat hundreds of square miles of Norwegian Sea.

The scale of the concrete gun mount in front of me finally crystalized, and Randi spoke my thoughts. "It could reach everything you see, everything."

This massive pedestal once supported one of the three "Adolph Guns" that formed Batterie Dietl. This was one of the largest land-based cannons in the entire world, hurdling a two-thousand-pound shell through a sixty-four-foot barrel out to thirty-five miles. The sheer scale of this weapon was terrifying, aptly matching the menacing structure we had just explored.

More solemnly, Batterie Dietl – as this menacing structure was known – was not unique. It was just one of the many coastal forts that Nazi Germany constructed to both deny the Norwegian Sea to the Allies and defend iron ore shipments coming south that, in turn, supplied the Nazi war effort throughout Europe.

As an American, we're taught the history of World War Two, but it's hardly present in our day-to-day landscape – especially where I grew up in the Midwest. There, we have no battlefields or ruins from this terrible time. But here, the beautiful Norwegian fjords are permanently scarred; war's dark mark etched into the rock like an enduring cave drawing, forever reminding everyone who looks just how close we came to the edge.

For Jonas and Randi, I could see these thoughts cloud their eyes as they remembered. Both their countries were invaded and occupied in that war, and their lives would have been shockingly different if events had taken a different course.

Randi may never have had the opportunity to summit Everest, and Jonas and I may never have had the chance to even visit this part of the world.

But the mood lightened as we slowly made our way back to the car – this time opting to trace the hill's curve along the shoreline instead of another damp trudge through the bunker. The dramatic greens and yellows of Engeløya came back into view, along with cheery red splashes from the occasional barn. Additionally, the returned sounds of coastal life and waves crashing onto the rocks added a breath of fresh air to what we'd just toured. A last glance back at the imposing grey structure reaffirmed that Randi's idea to stop here was a good one. History has so much to teach, I thought to myself, and it's worth remembering.

9

One Last Fire

Our lives on that remote island were busy. Boat runs to the mainland occurred daily, sometimes transporting guests and other times picking up the much anticipated and celebrated weekly grocery order. Meanwhile, on the island, everyone seemed to have settled into a somewhat isolated niche.

Jozef had his work restoring that old cabin with his ever-present sheep spectators. Ant had his pots and pans to attend to amid his constant fishing trips for his prized halibut. I had my newfound passion for guiding guests up in the mountains interspersed with my more regular routine of setting out breakfast, and the list went on for everyone.

Amid all these interwoven happenings, the island serenely weathered each day as a calm and steadfast haven in the Norwegian Sea. Jesper and Astrid were the image of unruffled organization. They presented each guest with the slow and peaceful island feeling visitors expected while seamlessly stoking the roaring steam engine in the background that kept everything running smoothly – and that was us.

But the more efficient we became at our tasks and keeping the island running, the less we saw of each other. The majority of our tasks were solo endeavors, and I only seemed to cross paths with my fellow travelers at mealtimes. A few of us would inevitably find ourselves admiring the ocean from the comfortable wooden chairs outside our cabin door in the evenings. Still, even then, we were always missing a friend or two to the island's endless evening chores.

For this reason, the handful of occasions where we had no guests on the island were transformed into a local holiday. Suddenly, there were no rooms to change over, no guests to cook for, and no clients for the guides to take out. These days were rare, however. So rare that I only remember one in particular.

Rumors had been flying this way and that for over a week. "Did you hear? There may be no guests this Friday." A hundred variations of that sentence circulated over meals and evening drinks. We didn't have much to gossip about in that remote corner of the world, so any exciting snippet of possibility was immediately seized and recirculated.

Therefore, Jesper seemed wholly unsurprised when the entire island population of ten gathered punctually and quietly for his regular morning visit. Over the weeks, we'd all grown criminally casual about those visits where Jesper dished out the daily tasks. We all knew what we had to do, and if there was any doubt, Jesper always scribbled the jobs on a little handheld whiteboard in our cabin. So why bother to roll out of bed as early as that maniacal workaholic?

But today was different, we all knew it, and Jesper knew it. So, he drew himself to his full daunting height with his curly black hair brushing the ceiling beams and took on a dramatic posture as if he were about to deliver grave news. "I'm sorry to say," he started while gazing solemnly at our smiling faces, "that we have no guests." The rumors were confirmed to a rousing cheer. "You all have the day off." Most of us stayed just long enough to hear him wish us a relaxing day before we began to scatter towards the kayaks and rock climbing gear. But his booming voice echoed through the house as we pulled on our shoes. "AND! We're having a bonfire on the beach tonight."

And then we were gone. The freedom of the day was a conglomerate of individual adventures. A couple of volunteers slid into their kayaks and took off for the day. Others commandeered the wood-fired hot tub for some much-needed relaxing. The rest, like myself, took the day to simply kick back, read, or catch up on writing – as was my case.

When evening approached, we slowly reconvened on the island's east side, facing the mainland, and scrounged enough wood together for a friendly little campfire on the rough sand. The evening was blissfully still. Hardly a cloud in the sky and barely a wisp of wind to ruffle the ocean that stood just a few paces from our fire. Across this water stood the impressive mountains of the mainland that glowed in the subtle pinks and purples of a fading day, courtesy of late summer beginning to offer a brief dusk before the sun rose again.

As the fire crackled healthily, our conversation naturally drifted toward plans. We were all traveling, and almost by definition, our life was ruled by plans and itineraries. Plans for where we were heading next, plans for what we were going to do once home, and plans for what job we wanted in the future – despite Jesper's playful promises to double our volunteer pay if we agreed to stay.

For some of us, myself included, future plans were still a little too far off to seriously consider. But for others, it was right in front of them as they prepared themselves for new adventures and journeys. Both Lydia, an energetic English woman from Manchester, and the French carpenter Jozef were scheduled to depart within the next two days, a sad aspect to making friends while traveling – we all need to say goodbye eventually.

We, therefore, took the evening for just as it was. Simply time to talk, laugh, reminisce, and enjoy each other's company and the near-impossible series of events that allowed our paths to cross in that remote corner of the Arctic.

Jesper was in the midst of relaying the saga of a particularly exacting Swedish guest when I spotted Astrid heading down to our breach from the main house with a guitar in hand. Until then, I had no knowledge of a guitar residing on the island nor that Astrid could play and sing pleasantly well. Therefore, I was surprised and infinitely pleased when she added her talents to that soft Norwegian evening.

During my three months on the island, I'd never had any remarkable adventures with Astrid. She very seldom joined us for the hiking or kayaking excursions off-island. But her supremely good cooking had endeared all of us volunteers to her before Ant had arrived to take over that role. Additionally, Astrid had been nursing a sourdough culture for years, from which she regularly baked loaves that I've never found an equal to on either side of the Atlantic. Like Jesper, she also possessed an infinitely kind and patient demeanor that undoubtedly helped them become the perfect couple for managing that remote lodge, and her long, dark blonde hair, vivid blue eyes, and friendly smile also made her the ideal stereotypical partner for Jesper's massive Nordic build.

We all heartily welcomed Astrid as she weaved through the group to sit in front of Jesper. Although I cannot remember the exact songs she played – save one – I do recall our smiling faces and the overwhelming feeling of contentment that settled over me that evening. The mountains, ocean, crackle of the fire, and tranquil sky created the perfect canvas of serenity, on which my new friends and I were simply small characters playing our part in that greater scene.

At about this time, Astrid drifted into a pleasant ditty concerning beards – an *Ode To Beards* from the musical duo Rocky and Balls – and I half listened to her soft singing while contemplating the many faces I'd grown accustomed to over those months.

> "There are beards that reach down to your toes,
> and beards that grow right up your nose."

Astrid sang in a beautiful voice partway between Scandinavian lullaby and American country.

Jozef was perched on a rock with a beer and his curly black hair for once free of sawdust. His scruff had continued to mature over the weeks, and his now-fledging jet-black beard matched his hair and oversized black sweatshirt to make a dark canvas that was only broken by his gleamingly perfect white smile. In fact, his smile is one of his most enduring traits that I remember after all these interceding years. No matter how frustrated he became with something not coming together in his carpentry endeavors, he could always lapse into that smile with a dramatic flourish of hand and call out in his French accent to let me know that "Ever-sing is oonder controol."

> "Some are big and some are small,
> And some men don't have one at all."

Astrid continued in the background while gazing at Jesper's full black beard that was just starting to curl at the edges.

Meanwhile, my fellow American Kelsy was perched on a stone with her knees drawn up under her chin as she gazed at the scenery with a contented smile. Her light brown hair was pulled back in a ponytail revealing her ever-present beaded necklace and youthful freckles, completing her classic southern country look that tracked perfectly with her North Carolina upbringing. I also smiled, remembering her tireless curiosity and remarkably accurate travel compass that could steer her to be in just the right place at the right time whenever an adventure was brewing. Kelsy was always there, from our paddle under the midnight sun to a heart-pounding cliffside trail run. They say spontaneity needs just a spark, and Kelsy's young, daring spirit was always ready to touch off an excursion of one kind or another.

> "Just the sight of a beard can cure a frown.
> Naked chins just leave me feeling down."

I was now captivated by Astrid's simple song, as were most of my companions, and a few threw me a mock frown and pointed to my perpetually naked chin.

Ola's broad shoulders filled his classic white T-shirt as he gazed serenely at the water. He'd become the defacto foreman for our little crew thanks to his perpetual relaxed and gentle approach to life and had helped with everything from preparing food to guiding guests on kayak trips around the islands.

His calm blue eyes and newly arriving crinkles hinted at his kind demeanor that his chiseled physique and serious-looking beard might otherwise overshadow. The newly arrived Nikolai was also cradling a beer as he patiently heard everyone's answer to how we all happened to come here.

Astrid's beautiful voice continued to waft through the air.

"My grandma had one I recall,
but ladies' beards aren't beautiful."

And, of course, Jesper's commanding presence could not be missed. He was situated on a gently sloping rock rising from the beach as Astrid sang away from her comfortable position in the sand just in front of him, using his chest for a backrest. His classic black and red flannel made him look remarkably like a bearded Nordic version of the Brawny Paper Towels mascot. But despite his intimidating size and equally daunting knowledge of the outdoors that I wished to learn, his unflappable friendliness was all I saw now. That tired smile that we all knew hid horrendously long work days as he toiled to build up that island lodge. But he was never too busy to care about us, his little fold of travelers, as he demonstrated now by taking the time to simply sit with us when every ounce of his will must have been screaming for sleep.

"And even though it's hard to hear.
I think I only love you for your beard."

Astrid finished, reaching up and giving Jesper's beard an affectionate tug. He responded by clapping his massive hands onto her slim shoulders and giving her a fond squeeze.

For once, I wasn't thinking about where I was going next. Or comparing this place to my memories of others. I was present, content, and pleased with where I was. These were the people who created that Norway trip for me over those three months. The faces and characters came and went, and, in truth, I cannot remember which of those faces actually attended that calm bonfire on the beach. Some may have already left the island to continue their travels. But in my memory, they were all there. Their smiles and stories forever melded with the overwhelming feeling of contentment I felt on that particular night.

This is what I started traveling for. To find those moments and scenes beyond what my desk was teaching me. And after all that had happened and all the firsts I'd encountered in Norway, I remember and cherish this most, a simple bonfire on the beach with the people that had made those experiences possible. There are countless sayings dictating how to act when happiness finds its way into your life, yet for me, it's simply to move over and look at what made it stop by. That night, as we swapped stories about kayaking through fjords and rappelling down mountains, it was clear that my lure for happiness was transforming what may have once seemed extraordinary at a desk in Minnesota into the ordinary.

We stayed out there as long as the ocean allowed. Until the tide's inevitable creep slowly began to make our fire sizzle in protest, and the orange embers flashed a warning that the evening was coming to an end. Indeed, the ocean would soon erase that fire from existence as if it had never happened, just as every single one of us would eventually disperse to carry on with our travels and leave that world behind. But that tiny spit of land off the coast of Northern Norway had changed everything, and its influence would shape everything that was to come. Later, that life change made me grin as I sat down at my computer looking for my next experience – and a promotion looking for volunteers to help guide trips in the Nicaraguan volcanoes suddenly looked remarkably appealing...

ABOUT THE AUTHOR

Daniel Purdy received a bachelor's degree in aerospace engineering from the Florida Institute of Technology. From there, he spent about three years working as a design engineer in Minnesota, first for a consulting company in Eden Prairie and later for an aircraft firm in Duluth. But his latent passion for the outdoors and travel materialized during a leave of absence trip to Norway. This launched him into a series of unique experiences, from guiding volcano trips in Nicaragua to looking after pumas and condors in Peru to hiking in the Himalayan Mountains, all of which have fueled his constant desire to explore and experience as much of the world as possible. But these travels also showed Daniel that his passion lies in guiding and opening the world for others. He now pursues that goal as a professional guide, first leading backpacking trips in Washington State and now as a bicycle guide for a Vermont-based company. In his off time, Daniel is always writing to inspire and encourage everyone to experience the world around them. But even between guiding and writing, he continues to travel and explore the world as much as possible.

Stay up to date with Daniel's latest travels and future book releases by following his Instagram @purdytravel.

9 781088 265222